EYE LEVEL

Winner of the Walt Whitman Award
of the Academy of American Poets

2017

Selected by Juan Felipe Herrera

Sponsored by the Academy of American Poets,
the Walt Whitman Award is given annually to the winner
of an open competition among American poets
who have not yet published a book of poems.

EYE LEVEL

POEMS

JENNY XIE

Graywolf Press

This publication is made possible, in part, by the voters of Minnesota through a Minnesota State Arts Board Operating Support grant, thanks to a legislative appropriation from the arts and cultural heritage fund, and a grant from the Wells Fargo Foundation. Significant support has also been provided by Target, the McKnight Foundation, the Lannan Foundation, the Amazon Literary Partnership, and other generous contributions from foundations, corporations, and individuals. To these organizations and individuals we offer our heartfelt thanks.

Published by Graywolf Press
212 Third Avenue North, Suite 485
Minneapolis, Minnesota 55401

www.graywolfpress.org

Published in the United States of America

ISBN 978-1-55597-802-0

6 8 10 12 11 9 7 5

Library of Congress Control Number: 2017938013

Cover design: Jeenee Lee Design

Cover art: Shen Wei, *Half Persimmon*, 2009. Copyright © Shen Wei. Courtesy of Flowers Gallery, London and New York.

For my family

CONTENTS

Rootless   1

•

Unspoiled Fictions   5
Phnom Penh Diptych: Wet Season   6
Phnom Penh Diptych: Dry Season   13
Corfu   19
Displacement   20
Fortified   21
Epistle   22

•

Old Wives' Tales on Which I Was Fed   25
Solitude Study   26
Zuihitsu   27
Alike, Yet Not Quite   30
Lunar New Year, 1988   31
Metamorphosis   34
Naturalization   35
Lineage   36
Chinatown Diptych   37

•

Origin Story   41

Captivity   42

Private Property   43

Invisible Relations   44

Bildungsroman   45

Visual Orders   46

Borderless   50

No Animal   51

Melancholia   52

Inwardly   53

Square Cells   54

Tending   55

Exit, Eve   60

•

Hardwired   63

The Hunt   64

Zazen   65

To Be a Good Buddhist Is Ensnarement   66

Margins   67

Déjà Vu   69

Letters to Du Fu   70

Exile   71

A Slow Way   72

Ongoing   73

Long Nights   74

Notes   79

*The eye you see is not
an eye because you see it;
it is an eye because it sees you.*
Antonio Machado

ROOTLESS

Between Hanoi and Sapa there are clean slabs of rice fields
and no two brick houses in a row.

I mean, no *three*—
See, counting's hard in half-sleep, and the rain pulls a sheet

over the sugar palms and their untroubled leaves.
Hours ago, I crossed a motorbike with a hog strapped to its seat,

the size of a date pit from a distance.
Can this solitude be rootless, unhooked from the ground?

No matter. The mind resides both inside and out.
It can think itself and think itself into existence.

I sponge off the eyes, no worse for wear.
My frugal mouth spends the only foreign words it owns.

At present, on this sleeper train, there's nowhere to arrive.
Me? I'm just here in my traveler's clothes, trying on each passing town for size.

UNSPOILED FICTIONS

"when the natives see you, the tourist, they envy you, they envy your ability to leave your own banality and boredom . . ." —Jamaica Kincaid

The ease with which a place becomes an entry:
searchlight   viewfinder   fantasy's aperture

Smell of my lateral gazing
Reach of the outsider's extravagant need

While I listened for the dialects
While I hunted down the night markets' chewed lips

Authentic encounters executed   *just so*
Extractions of color and details in the needed size

Beauty kept simple and numbness hot
The contrast and the rot in the air are merciful

PHNOM PENH DIPTYCH: WET SEASON

August, chambered. City of a million young faces.

A woman perches sidesaddle on a motorbike.
Another clutches stiff bread and leeks.

And how combed through, this rain!

The riled heat reaches the river shoal before it reaches the dark.

•

There's new money lapping at these streets.
Thirsts planted beneath the shells of high-rises.

Norodom Boulevard, flanked by stale bulbs,
lets through a motorcade.

 In the backseat of a gold Lexus
 a minister's son lies, his eyes shut
 dumb with honeyed sleep.

Fixtures: slack lips of suitcases, lukewarm showers up to three times in a day.
Mosquito bites on the arms and thighs, patterned like pips on dice.

An hour before midnight, the corners of the city begin to peel.
Alley of sex workers, tinny folk songs pushed through speakers.
Karaoke bars bracketed by vendors hawking salted crickets.

How do eyes and ears keep pace?

•

The zippered notes of bike engines enter
through an opening in my sleep.

My dreams sputtering out because of this.

It's useless to describe the slurry of humidity or the joy of a fistful of rice cradled in curry, but it's not that I'm at a loss for words.

Every day I drink Coca-Cola and write ad copy.
I'm in the business of multiplying needs.

Today, it's whitening face lotion, whitening foam wash, whitening sunscreen.
Across the seas, the copy can only read *brightening.*

But here, things blanch.

•

Desire makes beggars out of each and every one of us.

Cavity that cannot close.
That cracks open more distances.

A man whose outline I know
dives into a rooftop pool.
Rips a body-sized hole into it.

Wanting falls around me. Heavy garment.

After clocking out, a group of telecom managers tear into durians.

And now that the daylight turns viscous, a new wife buckles limbs
with a foreign lover at the Himawari Hotel.

Someone sweeps thick cockroaches from the floor, someone orders oysters on ice.

Even the rain sweats, unkempt like the rest of us.

•

I enter Wat Langka to sit.
To still the breath.
A steadying out and in, out and in.

Still, here in this country, something I can't ever enter.

On the screen: glow of missives.

Friends with pressed collars riding elevators.
They pass on left lanes, laboring in the din of American cities.

The stock market will dive spectacularly,
but no one yet knows this.

I'm still where I am, in conditions of low visibility.
Why not wait until I've waited *why* out?

•

The irony of the White Building is lost on no one.

It's a face repeatedly emptied by a fist.
It hangs on by dirtied rag, by pure stubbornness.

I've lived across from it, walked past neighbors
gambling on Nokia phones held together by elastic bands
and grandmothers fanning coals to smoke fish.

For my own apartment, I paid too much.
In the kitchen, I catch myself in a pan of water, but there I am transparent.

You could say moving here was a kind of hiding.

The compass needle points to where nothing begins.
I ride the cheapest forms of transportation,
my sight carries me just as far.

Yes, I'm tired of laundry soured by mildew.

This lonesomeness turning over
when it smells my approach.

•

Rainwater mars the tin roofs,
melts a sticky bun left in the alley.
It worries down the final tips of daylight.

How long will it be like this?

Water growing out of water.

The tourists curate vacation stories,
days summed up in a few lines.

Killing Fields tour, Sambo the elephant
in clotted street traffic,
dusky-complexioned children hesitant in their approach.

How the viewfinder slices the horizon—

Their pleasure is shrill, I agree.
It knows little of how banality
accrues with no visible evidence.

•

I wake up one morning to find beauty suspect.

Outside, a vendor hacks at a slab of ice
while two teenaged boys wait
for bags of crushed sugarcane juice
on matching motorbikes.

These commonplace nouns.

      A rain that chases
      the tail of my silence until sundown.

PHNOM PENH DIPTYCH: DRY SEASON

Motorbikes darting. Nattering horns leave an aftertaste.

I mark the distance on a map: this city a wrist-width away from the last.

Come sunrise, street dogs will turn their thoughts to wet foods.

It's not easy to measure your life in debts.

•

For years now, I've been using the wrong palette.
Each year with its itchy blue, as the bruise of solitude reaches its expiration date.

Planes and buses, guesthouse to guesthouse.

I've gotten to where I am by dint of my poor eyesight,
my overreactive motion sickness.

9 p.m., Hanoi's Old Quarter: duck porridge and plum wine.

Voices outside the door come to a soft boil.

I sweat over plates of pork dumplings and watery beer.

Can you fix this English?
the Chinese restaurant owner asks, pushing a menu toward me.

The men here chew toothpicks like uncles on both sides of my family.
They talk with their mouths full.

I translate what little I can, it's embarrassing.

Just passing through?
asks his eldest daughter, as she turns away to the fan.

•

My guilt goes off,
then returns, wilder.

For whom does it return?

All I do is recede from the view
of those at my back.

Heeding only the tug of the interior.

It's not about the snare of need, though I forget why I came.

Perhaps it's shallow sleep in the subtropics,
my youthful ambitions wet and slack.

I wring them out.

I want to remember this, though not with wistfulness.
I hang my expectations out on a string.

The city warms its tongue by not saying anything.

•

Wooden spirit houses on the road to Kampot spray-painted gold, capacious enough for a pot of incense, a rice bowl, and one can of Fanta.

Noon, white hour.

The outlines of bungalows in the distance—impossible to part the seen and unseen. What's here and what isn't.

The language behind this language cracks open, and my questions follow suit.

Months of medium-rare insomnia.

    Wine makes me confuse
    elation with clarity, and so I traverse
    the night market, my purse empty.

There goes the moon, hardening on a hot skillet.

    All that is untouchable as far as the eye can reach.

   •

I thought I owned my worries, but here I was only pulled along by the needle
of genetics, by my mother's tendency to pry at openings in her life.

Calls made from a booth where one pays by the minute.

I fail to mention the bite of my mistakes,
furnish stories with movement
and no shades of despair.

No, I didn't travel here for the lawlessness.

    I developed an appetite for elsewhere—

Beauty, too, can become oppressive if you let it,
but that's only if you stay long enough.

If you stay long enough,
the heat's fingers will touch everything
and the imprint will sting.

•

I kept twisting my face in bar bathrooms,
in wet markets, in strangers' arms.

And the years here—
they broke through barriers
one by one, in a kind of line.

Men and women came and went.
The city was dry, and then it wasn't.

•

I knelt to the passing time.

CORFU

To the north and to the west: dark tips of cypress. Corfu in the slow math of July, and this reservoir of fear running low. The island has two hard-boiled hills. The bus descends one of them, blaring folk ballads. Houses the color of custard, some burnt. A Greek Orthodox monastery where even female cats can't enter. I've never set foot on this island before, but all day a familiar version of this self insists like a plain sweat stain against my back.

Pickpocketed days ago in France, all my dollars and euros gone. Yesterday, I landed in an airport so small I could see from one end to the other.

I've grown lean from eating only the past.

One line through customs,
and the plane impossibly close to the sea.
No ceremony in any of it.

DISPLACEMENT

The woman by the soap stand with the low neckline is beside herself. Ecstasy, from the Greek *ekstasis*, meaning *to stand outside oneself.* Estranged. In Kerkyra, beneath chalky sun, I put down coins for ice coffee and a taste of kumquat liqueur. Her crying jags force me into attention.

Pain with solidity displaces. Joy to be sloughed, to be stranger to oneself. These patterns of movement are ancient. Later, in the harbor, the boat guide tells me that long before the debt crisis, fishermen on the island fled into the watery caves to escape their wives.

Crumbled rust on boat metal.
In order to dock the boat,
the fisherman throws all his weight against the line.

FORTIFIED

The Old Fortress in Corfu Town rests on a promontory, with Albania's mountains legible to the east. In the sixteenth century, the Venetians dug a moat to protect the fortress from the Turks. Today there's no sign of disorder, only the white sailboats of the rich moored in the quay like grains of rice.

Here, I am a face unknown, which swells my appetite for this island. Climb alone to the top to look down on pit-colored roofed verandas, the olive and the scrub. Doubtless our lives are solitary, but also the inverse.

On the bus ride back,
we pass a store named Ni Hao, selling pelts.
Hello in all directions.

EPISTLE

Eavesdropping on a mother
needling at her mule-brained son

stopping by the side of the road
to examine the dry socket of Agios Georgios

the root of this self-denial is long
all those years I was spared of seeing myself through myself

Now the stifling days disrobe
distance giving autonomy the arid space to grow

I'll rinse later this afternoon in the sea
then compose lines to you of reasonable length

to say the opening you left is wide enough for me
but I'm stunned to love aloneness

OLD WIVES' TALES ON WHICH I WAS FED

The number of rice grains left in your supper bowl
foretells how many pockmarks will appear on your lover's face

Sleeping on your back will flatten your head's shape
but sleep on your stomach and you'll induce nightmares

Eating the fat inside the crab sharpens the mind
so too with roe extracted from a steamed fish

Never let your feet touch cold water from the bathtub or the sea
on days when you're menstruating

Pinch the nose before age six when the cartilage is pliable
so the nasal bridge will grow narrow and high

Drift asleep with your hair wet
and you'll suffer from decades of migraines

You'll wreck your eyesight poring over pages in low light
but looking at all things green from a distance can coax it back

SOLITUDE STUDY

Times when I think a mind uncluttered with others
is the only condition for gentleness

or that memory sticks like cartilage
to the meat of those with the most words.

Yet I know we can hold more in us than we do
because the body is without core

and when I can no longer keep dividing
the odds are in my favor to strike it out alone.

Seeing the collars of this city open
I wish for higher meaning and its histrionics to cease.

If only the journey between two people
didn't take a lifetime.

ZUIHITSU

Sunday, awake with this headache. I pull apart the evening with a fork. White clot behind the eyes.

Someone once told me, *before and after is just another false binary.* The warmed-over bones of January. I had no passport. Beneath the stove, two mice made a paradise out of a button of peanut butter.

Suffering operates by its own logic. Its gropings and reversals. Ample, in ways that are exquisite. And how it leaves—not unlike how it arrives, without clear notice.

These days, I've had my fill of Chinatown and its wet markets. Gutted fish. Overcooked chattering. The stench making me look hard at everything.

Summer mornings before the heat has moved in. Joy has been buried in me overnight, but builds in the early hours. My attention elastic.

The babbling streets of Causeway Bay, out of which the sharp taste of the city emerges. Nothing can stay dry here. The dark cherries of eyes come and go, as they please.

Let there be no more braiding of words. I want a spare mouth.

My father taught me wherever you are, always be looking for a way out: this opening or that one. Or a question. Sharp enough to slice a hole for you to slip through.

Long car trips where I sat in the back of our family's used Nissan. The stale odor of plush seats and sun-warmed cola. My parents' and my words do not touch. I grow adept at tunneling inward, a habit I have yet to let go of.

I am protective of what eyes cannot pry open. The unannounced. The infinite places within language to hide.

A Zen priest once told me that without snagging on a storyline, the body can only take loss for ninety seconds. The physical body has its limits, is what I heard. The imagination can break through them.

Boiled peanuts. Leather of daybreak. Cotton thinning out into thread. Dried vomit. Ice water from the spigot. The sacred and profane share a border. In the desert, small droppings of unknown origin.

Even when I was young, I loved peering at faces in films. The pleasure of watching and of not being watched.

Black koi fish open their mouths at the skin of the pond for oxygen. At the edge of the water, I hold two lines from Ikkyū in my mouth. Make my way slowly.

Nights when I shared a bed in a small room. Another's body to the left, hooked by a heavy dream.

Funny, the way we come to understand a place by wanting to escape it.

I can shake out the imprint of my body on the sheets each morning. Harder to shake out the mind.

When I was four, I ate spoonfuls of powdered milk straight from the canister. The powder was sweet. There wasn't enough money for fresh milk. Seven hundred years ago, Chang Yang-hao wrote, *All my life seems / like yesterday morning.*

ALIKE, YET NOT QUITE

After Li Shangyin

Thin fish bones arranged on the bone plate, a bracelet

Blushing after wine and high sun

The Buddhist nun, like a tipped glass, emptying through the mouth

Smell of shadows in both March and October

Solitude and coarse wanting, wedged stubbornly

The railway conductor's face, blank as the underside of a river

Paper gown at the gynecologist's office, onion skin, easy to part

Unhurried, the knife against the vegetable or the meat

Astonishment of being left and of choosing to leave

LUNAR NEW YEAR, 1988

Doors plastered with red paper cutouts
so that the oncoming year passes these houses by.

Sweep out the insistent winter.

Make what you will out of ritual—
the relative with the steadiest hands cuts the hair of her cousins.

·

Grain alcohol in a thimble glass.

The wife bleaches out the urine smell from the bathroom tile
while suffering the clean cuts of an insult.

And the husband?
He's out in the yard sucking on his cigarettes
and pondering prime numbers.

This year, a cluster of buildings in Hefei grew more buildings.

·

Everyone is pleased by a story of plenty.

The husband and the brother-in-law remove every item from the refrigerator
and arrange it all on the old card table for a Kodak photo.

It's the first point-and-shoot in the neighborhood.

The iron-rich spinach and clementines loose in their skins.
One bottle of artificial mango drink for show.

How quickly a photograph can erase all labor.
It says: we are sated, but the watercress and the pork are unending.

Frugality and daily rationing cropped out.

The camera neuters the present, so what becomes past cannot breed.

•

Envelopes arrive from a university overseas,
a new life activated.

The husband will go first. He purchases the family's only suitcase.

Already he knows when he boards the plane
this city will appear small, as will his life.

His clothing, moreover, will mark him
as someone who had to earn his way.

.

Even what hasn't yet cracked into being
can at any time exert its pull.

The whole neighborhood emerges at dusk.

Wakefulness drawn from the red applause
of firecrackers.

In the alleyway of my childhood home,
you can see I'm covering my ears.

At my back:
the years ahead, strangely lit.

METAMORPHOSIS

Nowhere in those kerosene years
could she find a soft-headed match.

The wife crosses over an ocean, red-faced and cheerless.
Trades the pad of a stethoscope for a dining-hall spatula.

Life is two choices, she thinks:
you hatch a life, or you pass through one.

Photographs of a child swaddled in layers arrive by post.
Money doesn't, to her embarrassment.

Over time, she grows out her hair. Then she sprouts nerves.
The wife was no fool, but neither did she wander.

She lives inside a season of thrift, which stretches on.
Her sorrow has thickness and a certain sheen.

The wife knows to hurry when she washes.
When she cooks, she licks spoons slowly.

Every night, she made a dish with ground pork.
Paired with a dish that was fibrous.

NATURALIZATION

His tongue shorn, father confuses
snacks for *snakes*, *kitchen* for *chicken*.
It is 1992. Weekends, we paw at cheap
silverware at yard sales. I am told by mother
to keep our telephone number close,
my beaded coin purse closer. I do this.
The years are slow to pass, heavy footed.
Because the visits are frequent, we memorize
shame's numbing stench. I nurse nosebleeds,
run up and down stairways, chew the wind.
Such were the times. All of us nearsighted.
Grandmother prays for fortune
to keep us around and on a short leash.
The new country is ill fitting, lined
with cheap polyester, soiled at the sleeves.

LINEAGE

One of the sent-down rusticated youth

Xia xiang: shuttled to the villages to work a steamed pot of land

Her austere fatigues and chatty pigtails

She learned to grin as the poster girls did, as if treating everyone out

Body doubled over under the basin of the sun

No books, just somatic pain that rings outward

Weak congee in the mornings, six girls to a room

Where to spend her astonishment, cursed with a short half-life

It was the border of adulthood, those fallow years

Even then she understood the living carry on by being fluid

And that there would be a child

And the child's face would sting of her own

CHINATOWN DIPTYCH

I.

The face of Chinatown returns its color,
plucked from July's industrial steamer.

Dry the cup!
So we do.

Four noodle shops on East Broadway release their belches collectively.
They breed in me a hankering for family life.

Here, there's no logic to melons and spring onions exchanging hands.
No rhythm to men's briefs clothes-pinned to the fire escape.

Retirees beneath the Manhattan Bridge leak hearsay.

The woman in Apartment #18 on Bayard washes her feet in pot of boiled
water each evening before bedtime. But every handful of weeks she lapses.

I lean into the throat of summer.

Perched above these streets with whom I share verbs and adjectives.

II.

Faces knotted, bangs softened with grease.
The East River pulls along a thread of sun.

While Sunday slides in. Again, in those plain trousers.

How the heat is driven off course.
How one can make out the clarified vowels of bridges.

Who's keeping count of what's given against what's stolen?

There's nothing I can't trace back to my coarse immigrant blood.

Uncles tipple wine on the streets of Mott and Bayard.
Night shifts meet day shifts in passing.

Sweat seasons the body that labors.

And in each noodle shop, bowls dusted with salt.

ORIGIN STORY

I was profligate like a floodlight to the sun.

Hoarded saccharine and toothmarks,
wanted only the thickest rhymes, two of each.

Full I was of promises I never intended to keep:
puckered laughter, lines to feast.

I let everyone who entered my life enter through me.
Demanded nonsense love and bodies that would ring.

Not to mention higher kilowatts
of creeping joy, more red in everything—

CAPTIVITY

Sleep is a narrow corridor. Even idleness will tire, forcing the mind to burrow into its emptiness. We said untrue things to make the time go faster, our teeth bright with holes. Nights, sentences clattered in us until they didn't. I'd forgotten all about humiliation. And yet another month fattened, tightening at the seams. It wasn't clear if there was an outside world to our outside world. Every few weeks, voices leaked in from the windows. Other times, kernels of rainwater and ice.

PRIVATE PROPERTY

Exhaustion slides from the body through the lips first. The invisible are flush with it, they drowse on blue subway seats. Heads bowed, yes, but to what. This island of concrete and glass tied by rough hands. The smell of this body among other bodies. Negatives of another's pleasure. All of us living on loan—yet only some grasp the arrangement. Those shuttled back and forth, drifting to other far places. Underground, the window is also a mirror. It reflects sleep chasing bodies back into the borderless empire of the interior.

INVISIBLE RELATIONS

There are no simple stories, because language forces distances. The days gummy and without drink. And a question stammers in the mind for weeks, one key aquiver on the piano. In the course of a day, your head will point in all the cardinal directions. It is good to wake and sleep, to scrape jars with spoons. Nights, grape popsicles sew sugar into your mouth. Police sirens clean the air and the TV burns out. Without your knowing, the unseen borders of your hunger are redrawn.

Far off, you are being stitched into a storyline in the smooth lobe of another's mind.

BILDUNGSROMAN

When the gates opened, some of us remained still. Others walked off, with no one to call after them. What a sight it was. You plant an alphabet in your sleep and wake to acres and acres of radios. Something long shuttered cracked. Faces no longer guileless. We felt time segmenting like lichens, a shade of ourselves quickening. In front of our eyes, the wind whipped its subjects forth in tune with some strange choreography. You could walk into a name for yourself. You could walk into a fear of being robbed of your life.

VISUAL ORDERS

[1]

Harvest the eyes from the ocular cavities.
Complete in themselves:
a pair of globes with their own meridians.

[2]

What atrophies without the tending of a gaze? The visible object is constituted
by sight. But where to spend one's sight, a soft currency? To be profligate in
taking in the outer world is to shortchange the interior one.

Though this assumes a clean separation, a zero-sum game.

[3]

To draw ink-lines across the lids
To dip into small pots of pigment
To brush two dozen times
To flush with water and tame with oil
To restrain and to spill in appropriate measure
To drink from the soft and silvery pane
To extract the root of the solitary so as to appear

[4]

Describe how the interior looks.
Cloak the eyes.
Close them, and seeing continues.

[5]

The seductions of seeing ensure there is that which remains unseen. Evading visibility is its own fortune. If to behold is to possess, to be looked upon is to be fixed in another's sight, static and immutable.

[6]

She leans toward the mirror for self-study.
The body canted.
What gets left out?
Uneasy depths.
The fine, lithe needles of the mind.
Endless conversation with no listener.

[7]

Self-consciousness anticipates an excess of seeing. Its incessancy.

Lacan writes, "I see only from one point, but in my existence I am looked at from all sides."

[8]

Gazed upon
I lose union with the larger surround
Broken from the trance of camouflage

[9]

The acquisitive, insatiable *I*.
A disembodied eye cannot be confined
to the skin and to what it holds captive.

Inversely, to be unseen against one's will is to be powerless.
To be denied a reflection and to be locked out of a self.

[10]

What persists down the generations?
The shape of the eyeball, translated by genes.
Mine are long like my mother's and her mother's—who was all but blind.

[11]

Ancient optic theory dictates that the eye sends out rays, which touches the object of sight. When the visual ray returns to the eye, the image is impressed on the mind. To see, then, was tactile.

That we are touchable makes us seen.

[12]

Sight is bounded by the eyes,
making seeing a steady loss.

The presence of the unseen is vaster
than that which is exhausted by vision.

We inhabit this incoherence.

[13]

Look at how I perform for you
Look at how you perform for me

An eye for an eye
is how you and I
take on forms in the mind

[14]

Her gaze breaks each time
at the same place.

There is no reversing—
didn't she know?

She has to go at it from the side.
She has to keep circling.

BORDERLESS

I.

On the night train
cherries wrapped
in newspaper crackle red:
shame's counterpoint.

The blood beneath my skin
and the blood beneath yours
wear each other out.

II.

February's malice—
from the window
I spot a fox cutting
across the snow.

A lone blade.
It startled.

No, it was chased.

III.

Everything is mind.

The fox and the cherry,
the shame and the blade.

Even the mouth of the outer world
sipping gingerly
on the broth of us.

NO ANIMAL

Two bucks approach the backyard, snouts grazing the chicory.

Where is my oblivion?

    Here I am: barefoot and shadow-cropped
    on the porch, rote on the phone.

Last summer, I painted the wood I stood on the color of eggs,
thinking the coat would last.

        This season a rash of mildew inflames the lowest planks.

        There go the pair! White tails studding the thicket.
            Emptied of the embarrassment of need.

I stay behind.
The present tense gets close, but doesn't enter me.

MELANCHOLIA

The black dog approaches?

      I pry open the crooked jaw.

Inside?

      A heady odor, elemental.

And then?

      I spin through my life again.

How so?

      Slow and fast, fast and slow.

What follows?

      Time, the oil of it.

What direction?

      Solitude throws me off the scent.

And what lies ahead?

      Even the future recoils, long as it is.

What points the finger?

      All of my eye's mistakes.

And what were they?

      Level.

INWARDLY

The lightest realizations arrive in restraint—
so the old masters tell us.

Not unlike the tug at the end of a line.

                              We have language for what is within reach
                                but not the mutable form behind it.

                                          Or else, why write.

I'm sick of peering at the ego.
No, my ego's tired of peering at *me*—

It's she who awakens me into being.

So it goes: the seer mistaken for the seen.

SQUARE CELLS

The screens plant bulbs
of tension inward, but hit no nerves.

River of speechless current.
My gaze faces the screen, laps up

blue-eyed policemen in bloom
and a fat fog fanning out by the inch

across cities in eastern China.
Refresh for a politician yawning

wolfish monosyllables.
In the bed of pixels, I can make out

truth and fiction taking turns,
one imitating the other.

My window faces stone and glass.
My screen faces my face.

Today the clean square cells of this city
contain so many faces.

Each brightened by a fear
which makes them commonplace.

TENDING

The storm's cracked.

Tracks of some animal
has spackled ant holes
hidden beneath a bed of grass.

       And what now—

Rain stains everything.

     Water pulls off the blindfold.
     Draws forth what's been planted.

Hours ago, the sky was stupored—

and the mouth of May, slow peach.

It's past the hour
when larkspurs leak
poisonous alkaloid seeds.

Danger coils here, too.

Kudzu can smother up to a foot a day.

A walk through the garden
sets off the mind's tripwires.

This year, the wisteria murmur.
Then ring, out of season.

The light: raucous
or the light: slow and scummed.

Which is it?

One hour loosens
from the socket of another.

The rain's not yet done, but the light
            comes feeling

its way back,

            as it does.

The interior smells fecund.

But this greening's abbreviated
by the carbon blade of shears.

One self prunes violently
at all the others
thinking she's the gardener.

Even so, the blossoms drip.
     Spill over.
               A few inches above, the sticky murmur of flies.

     Disorder begins to flare.

          There are roots long in the earth, and they hasten.

     And pink worms, out of sight,
              with their dim impulse
       to let the dirt churn through them.

EXIT, EVE

I cut my teeth on green flesh   Eden's navel

Now I understand our vocabulary   for what astounds us is thin

    •

Red ginger flower   nature doesn't hide its excess

Fear lifts a bone from its mouth   nature is exact like this

    •

Lately I eat soft fruits   and plain speech

Like a mule   I understand one suffers by the load one chooses

    •

It just so happens that I write lines   that men leave well alone

This flat blaze of fury   simplifies me

    •

I'll leave tomorrow   traversing the side roads

Let everyone see   no one paid my way

HARDWIRED

A misfortune can swell
for a long, long time in the mind.

While goodness shrinks
down to a hard shell.

I reach for the hammer,
but it doesn't crack.

Evolutionarily, it makes sense.

These fishbone days, this fatty grief.

THE HUNT

Ferried over to the banks of the present:
the life that outgrew this one.

As fate would have it
the ungovernable remained ungovernable.

Love's laws are simple. The leaving take the lead.
The left-for takes a knife to the knots of narrative.

Make no mistake: one cannot cover distance with more distance.

Would it be accurate to say that ownership robbed her of labor?
That the labor injected color into lust?

She always knew all wanting is setting out
on the trail of your own flickering scent.

The body taking up the gait of a bloodhound.

ZAZEN

Sour tobacco, tofu bowl, bright.
Planks of hollyhock in Anhui,
the way *I don't know* could open
months later like a hive.
Hard tide of shame that I thought
had dried out years ago.
Love's barks grow watery, faint.
I walk the edge of an honest life.
The lash of carnal thoughts, followed
by the thin whip of banal guilt.
Seed of an itch on the left foot sole.
Hot yellow lights of cities
where I once pressed, over and over,
up against alternate lives.

Now, I sit. Above a deep ground.
The mind fetches the chatter.

And so on, and so forth.

TO BE A GOOD BUDDHIST IS ENSNAREMENT

The Zen priest says I am everything I am not.

In order to stop resisting, I must not attempt to stop resisting.

I must believe there is no need to believe in thoughts.

Oblivious to appetites that appear to be exits, and also entrances.

What is there to hoard when the worldly realm has no permanent vacancies?

Ten years I've taken to this mind fasting.

My shadow these days is bare.

It drives a stranger, a good fool.

Nothing can surprise.

Clarity is just questioning having eaten its fill.

MARGINS

Water striders on a pond's surface,
light as calipers:
long sentence for which there are no words.

  •

Indoors, silence travels from west to east.
The house I keep
no monastery.

  •

Tsvetaeva, open on my bedside table.
Lines feeding on a crust
of lamplight.

  •

A monk brushes crumbs from the cushion.
In the meditation hall, the sound of bells.
Thinner than any keyhole.

·

Hard to tune
the last decade of my life.
January, few visitors.

·

Each day mostly like any other.
The way you loved me, a cracked wind
hurrying me along.

DÉJÀ VU

Odd number of women trimming their face
hairs with tiny scissors. They catch themselves
in their mirrors, sip the day languorously.
Noon in Jardín Centenario is creased.

Between them pass words and murmurs
that fasten quite close to the ground.

Every now and then
a thought rips into being—
most relations with the self are facsimile.

Is it when pain is sincere
so as to be unrecognizable
that little static
from the original comes through?

Though who's to say even this is new.

LETTERS TO DU FU

I paid a visit to the province of a past year   aided by a pot of wine
Self-contempt erects a wide frame   almost anyone can pass through

So unruly are my needs   who would own up to it
Only a fool would try to imitate the arrow   before letting go the bow

•

Du Fu, do not attempt this journeying   with a whip of effort
To speed up your travel   step backward into the broad forgetting

They say too much brooding   elongates the mind
Everywhere one lands   the train arrives at the depot early or late

•

Fruitless to try and compare   your searching lines
with the rain's heavy lather   I'll take instead the shaved surface of the moon

We are wiped of age first thing in the morning   sleep is a light wash
and don't we know it   we are wrung and wrung

EXILE

Here's to this new country:
bald and without center.

To its paper rooftops
and dogs pink with mange.

To pain, which cleans
out everything:
the fantasies that wouldn't take,
ancient mistakes.

Here's to the north and south
of this lack and its mud.
I feel my way around.

To new nouns.

To burning off
like soft, white butter
set in a saucepan.

A SLOW WAY

It's possible I'm tallying
wrong in this life.

Better to count down than up.

I only have to shuck off
these other minds
to reach the first mind.

The one that stores nothing.
Coming before and after.

The simplicity of it is difficult.

Suffering lies here in the open
but doesn't belong to anyone.

It migrates laterally.
A slow way—
exchanging hands.

ONGOING

Never mind the distances traveled, the companion
she made of herself. The threadbare twenties not
to be underestimated. A wild depression that ripped
from January into April. And still she sprouts an appetite.
Insisting on edges and cores, when there were none.
Relationships annealed through shared ambivalences.
Pages that steadied her. Books that prowled her
until the hard daybreak, and for months after.
Separating new vows from the old, like laundry whites.
Small losses jammed together so as to gather mass.
Stored generations of filtered quietude.
And some stubbornness. Tangles along the way
the comb-teeth of the mind had to bite through, but for what.
She had trained herself to look for answers at eye level,
but they were lower, they were changing all the time.

LONG NIGHTS

Ice, entire cakes of it.
Crows feed on sand.

So poor is this season
the ground steals color
from the tree-shadows.

•

Can it be that nothing
is as far as here?

Just look!

How much past we have
to cover this evening—

•

Come to think of it
don't forget to pick
off this self and that self
along the way.

Though that's not right—
You spit them out like pits.

•

If there is a partition between
the outer and inner worlds,
how is it that some water in me churns
between the mountain ranges?

How is it we are absorbed so easily
by the ground—

•

Long nights for simple words.

•

Slant rhyme of current thinking
and past thinking.

A chewed-over hour, late.
Where the long-ago past
and the future come
to settle scores.

•

Traveling and traveling,
but so much interior
unpicked over by the eyes.

•

Nothing is as far as here.

NOTES

The epigraph for the book comes from *Times Alone: Selected Poems of Antonio Machado*, translated by Robert Bly (Wesleyan University Press, 1983).

The epigraph for "Unspoiled Fictions" comes from Jamaica Kincaid's *A Small Place* (Farrar, Straus and Giroux, 2000).

"Solitude Study" borrows a phrase from an essay by Jeffrey Weiss in *On Kawara—Silence*, a catalog published in conjunction with an exhibition of Kawara's work in the Solomon R. Guggenheim Museum, New York.

"Zuihitsu" quotes a line from Chang Yang-hao's "Four Verses," which appears in *The Shambhala Anthology of Chinese Poetry*, translated and edited by J.P. Seaton (Shambhala Press, 2006).

"Alike, Yet Not Quite" borrows its form from "Resemblances" by Li Shangyin from *Derangements of My Contemporaries: Miscellaneous Notes*, translated by Chloe Garcia Roberts (New Directions, 2014).

The last two lines of "Lunar New Year, 1988" play with the Chinese temporal term for *after/later* (hòu), which shares the same character as the Chinese spatial term for *back/rear*.

In "Lineage," *xia xiang* ("down to the countryside") is a Chinese term for the mass transfer of urban Chinese youth to the rural countryside during the Cultural Revolution as part of the government's rustication policy.

In "Visual Orders," the line by Jacques Lacan comes from *The Four Fundamental Concepts of Psycho-Analysis* (Norton, 1978).

In "The Hunt," the line "The leaving take the lead" is adapted from two lines in Martine Bellen's "Reprise Dream" from *Tales of Murasaki and Other Poems* (Sun & Moon Press, 2000).

ACKNOWLEDGMENTS

Grateful acknowledgment is made to the editors of the following publications, where these poems, some in earlier versions and under different titles, originally appeared: The Academy of American Poets' "Poem-a-Day," the *American Poetry Review*, *American Poets*, *Columbia: A Journal of Arts & Literature*, *cream city review*, *Day One*, *Gulf Coast*, *Harvard Review*, *Hayden's Ferry Review*, *Kenyon Review Online*, the *Literary Review*, *Meridian*, *Narrative*, the *New Republic*, *Oxford Poetry*, *Pleiades*, *Poetry*, *Salt Hill*, *Tin House*, *Washington Square Review*, and ZYZZYVA.

•

"Hardwired" was featured in *Poetry Daily*. "Zuihitsu" was republished in the *Brooklyn Poets Anthology*. "Private Property" was written in response to Emma Lazarus's "The New Colossus" as part of the 92nd Street Y Unterberg Poetry Center's *A New Colossus* festival. A selection of these poems appear in *Nowhere to Arrive*, winner of the 2016 Drinking Gourd Chapbook Prize, published by Northwestern University Press.

•

Deep gratitude to the following organizations and institutions for their generous support and community: the English and creative writing departments at Princeton University, the Creative Writing Program at New York University, Kundiman, the Elizabeth George Foundation, Provincetown Fine Arts Work Center, Poets & Writers, Cave Canem's Writing Across Cultures workshops, Brooklyn Zen Center, and the Academy of American Poets.

It is a joy to thank my teachers: Eduardo C. Corral, Suezette Given, Rigoberto Gonzáles, Yusef Komunkayaa, Deborah Landau, Sharon Olds, Meghan O'Rourke, Rebecca Rainof, James Richardson, Brenda Shaughnessy, Tracy K. Smith, Craig Morgan Teicher, C.K. Williams, and Rachel Zucker.

Enormous gratitude to the Academy of American Poets and to Juan Felipe Herrera, whom I cannot thank enough.

Jeff Shotts and the superlative Graywolf team: it is a thrill and privilege to work with you.

Abiding thanks to my friends and loved ones, many more than can be named here. I'm especially grateful for the following individuals for their kinship and for their hand in helping shape some of these poems: Kaveh Akbar, Abba Belgrave, Amanda Calderón, Elysha Chang, Cathy Linh Che, DéLana Demaron, Jameson Fitzpatrick, Hafizah Geter, Marwa Helal, Sophie Herron, Jen Hyde, Vt Hung, Dana Isokawa, Mike Lala, Robin Coste Lewis, Peter Longofono, Ricardo Maldonado, Chrissy Malvasi, Virginia McClure, Amy Meng, Ansley Moon, Sahar Muradi, James O'Toole, Amy Paeth, Soham Patel, Allyson Paty, Kim Philley, Maya Popa, Cat Richardson, Sahar Romani, Nicole Sealey, Charif Shanahan, Jeannie Vanasco, and Marina Weiss.

Special thanks to Lizzie Harris, Jen Levitt, and Ben Purkert for indispensable readings of early drafts.

Boundless thanks to Ravi Shroff for the encouragement and support, and much else.

Thanks most of all to my family—from this shore to the next. My debt to you is everywhere in these pages.

JENNY XIE was born in Anhui, China, and resides in New York City. She is the author of two poetry collections: *Eye Level*, which was a finalist for the National Book Award and recipient of the Walt Whitman Award of the Academy of American Poets and the Holmes National Poetry Prize; and *The Rupture Tense*, which was also a finalist for the National Book Award. Her chapbook, *Nowhere to Arrive*, received the Drinking Gourd Prize. She has taught at Princeton University and NYU, and is currently on faculty at Bard College.

The text of *Eye Level* is set in Sabon MT Pro.
Book design by Rachel Holscher.
Composition by Bookmobile Design & Digital
Publisher Services, Minneapolis, Minnesota.
Manufactured by Versa Press on acid-free,
30 percent postconsumer wastepaper.